(www.reesispositive.com)

For Ourself

Contents

theories of the self

relationships

vulnerability

addiction

spirit

truth

soul

THE VANITY of humanity,
Inescapable boil of insanity,
Going 'out of our mind'
The blind leading the blind
Blind games.

The emancipation of alliteration,
procrastination manifest nation
Analysis paralysis with nom demarkation

Scrape the dotted landscape of your mind's eye,
Demystify the liquid lens,
Imbue the hue, enlighten friends,
Inhale for breath, or death at most,
(delivered by the demon host)
will make you go around the Benz

De-clamorize the false-glamorized perceived into the glow,
Just know,
Be known,
Less personality full-blown.

Brene Brown had it right... to a point,
Nebulize deeper to the ball joint,
Anoint the self intended, befriended mended regard for self,
Re-shelf.
Man-counts. A trans-actual amounts. His vanity.
Impure adulterated self-hated gestated impregnated vegetated outside the insanity.

Re-Perceive the iris,
Re account the soul,
Flow, grow, outwardly lose control.
The Know-Ledge of self perception... sub-concious self rejection,
Until we hedge our bets and frets and stew then strand it through...
To what we don't recall but always new.
The Knew Ledge.

Should I write about what I know?

Write about what you care about, nobody cares what you know.

past

Twisted Tutorials

Disneyland can be taxing,

If the nanny is not accounted for,

Vacations in absurd locations,

Parked in hotel rooms with isolating themes,

Matriarchal focus on hierarchical hocus pocus,

Concealing feelings in ritual, habitual, stitched up vitriol.

Sex control, mind games,

Anal retentive sugar coated treats, under the sheets,

Bloated, thrilled to bits,

Waiting in line to be scared out of wits.

Intemperate grooming of mother's nature,

Raging storm clouds house killer instincts

Nurtured by the pathetic patriarchal gunslinger

Unable to pull the triggers I now live with.

Twisted tutorials of stimulating lessons,

Exhilarating rides through a maze of textbooks.

Disneyland can be taxing,

If the nanny is not accounted for.

Terrible Children

Let tears of joy be window shield cleansers to the world of wonders,
Let them bake and cake and remind of souls of every naive breath we took,

Every move we make of innocence at once lost

All at once tossed on the unfettered scrapheap of the primitive machinations of my shame based wastelands
For thine eyes have seen the wonder in terrible children.

Lived the pitiful journey to a lifetime's suffering of being a human man being,

Only after tomorrow has passed onto the pages of pain will the rapture of the forgotten full force of naturalist parental humanity re-write the lessons un-learned.

A kindred spirit for the welfare of the state of affairs,
Treasure trove and re-chested for the least invested.

It was the worst of times,
It was the moving spectacle of crimes,
In the most recent of relational primitive prime-times.

My windshield to the world has wiped,
Cleaned the less-mourned memories,
Of terrible children.

Mind Bands

Invisible strands of mind stretching fantastic elastic mind bands

The Memory Shelf

I have recently become aquatinted with myself
Placed all my thoughts and memories upon a memory shelf
Deep see diving into recesses of Rees
Piece by painful piece
Seeking peace
To unpack what's underneath
To see what's submerged
And what comes up to the surface.
Delving deep into the ocean of my mind
Riding waves of length
Discovering a mental health
A treasured wealth
A salvage mission for myself
To get connected with my own authentic self
To tune into the memories upon my memory shelf

This changeful self-reflection was a choice
Though painful it has helped me find my true authentic voice

I came to realize, through real eyes, the real lies of my past
And though the see was vast, I worked them out at longest last,

All my life I presented
And what I re-presented
I resented
Put the kettle on, I'll make a brew of discontented
Awake a new, to stew,
On how to get through
When there's no way around
You've gotta get into it

To get over it

To get through it

When you can't bear it, share it

If you can't control it, let it go

When you can't feel it, have faith it exists

When you can't hold on, release it... into the abyss.

And when you find yourself fighting for your life, surrender, for you have already found yourself,

Inside the thoughts and memories upon your memory shelf.

Positivasaurus

Come ride the Positivasaurus,

A dinosaur for the negative in all of us.

Peace-meal creation,

Horton hears a who?

Horton seize the what?

Animalistic play,

Fighting the Cassius in the Clay,

That somebody threw away.

A pre-historic pre-dawn chorus,

Of the Positivasaurus.

Come ride the Positivasaurus,

A dinosaur for the negative in all of us.

Love's Last Stand

Eclectic, concentric, eccentric forts,
Of Electrified fences,
Defended senses,
Fears attack relentless.
Love's Last Stand.

Mustering,
A General Custering of courage,
Robert E. Lee-ving doubts at the castle gates,
Ulysses Grant-ing humanity hope,
Churchillien resilience,
In fields of human conflict,
Conscripting the constructs of
Freshly erected thoughts,
Eclectic, concentric, eccentric forts,
With Electrified fences,
Defended senses,
Fears attacked relentless,
Love's Last Stand.

I wasn't your first kiss,
The reason for your first bliss,
Your first hand held,
Your first heart swelled,
But let me be your last,
Lay down the ghosts and memories
Of all relations past.

Together now,

In this moment,

We adventure hand in hand

To a place of endings happiest,

Our world of Love's Last Stand.

Yesterday's Playroom

There's always room to laugh,

To play,

To live and love.

Always room to roam

Hide inside,

Reside outside,

Yesterday's playroom.

Sweep the syrupy sweet dusty cobwebs from the vintage toy-chest,

Least invested in,

Less I still be interested in.

Side by side,

We rode,

Trojan toys,

A past trapped and scrapped,

Piled up pillows dwell nested in gentle pillars, of

Yesterday's Playroom.

The in-appropriations committee walls of political rooms of play,

Crushing constricted constructs,

Of brain crashing waves,

Tarnished,
With moribund murky greyed remembrance
Of stolen hop-scotch,
On battlefields of forgotten toy soldiers, in
Yesterday's Playroom.

Storminess shelter,
Of the raging splintered music box in my mind,
Winds me up.

Salad days over,
Tossed up, un-dressed,
Served to re-assess,
Messes left best left,
To reside inside,

Yesterday's playroom

Asymmetrical

The most beautiful things are slightly asymmetrical,
Wilted, stilted, off kilter.
Imagined imperfections of fractured perceptions,
Broken together by sticky situations,
Floored ceilings of imagination,

Creations re-imagined,
Grown out of the stunted, shunted and maligned misaligned notions,
Of our imperviousness mind set
In porous, paradoxical loop the loops.
Harness the rough edges of the brain strand-scape,
Climatize calm,
Prioritize grace,

7

Chase the maze of hazy dayze from the head-space.

Gestate great,

Ingrain gain,

Grow the flow to a graduate class,

Realize the size to a physical mass,

Force not the natural course,

Of even(t)s and odd-vents,

Beholden is the golden radiant beauty,

Of history's briefest moments,

Brought forth from the time-scape,

Leaping into untreated, repeated heapings of

Lulled inaction,

Infractions distracted,

Protracted enacted detractions,

Dissatisfaction that 'You can't get no satisfactions'

From days malaise,

Hazy high-jinks invoked in daily, crazy avoidance,

Of what is, and what is knotted,

Sunk in deep trauma pockets full of change,

Hung up on anorexic mannequins,

Wearing threadbare and thin.

G(r)owing without,

Staining within,

Dormant in the beauty of the wilted, stilted, off kilter,

The most beautiful things are slightly asymmetrical.

Reality Bias

Our past can dictate our future present,
If we let it.
Our future's encumbered by greedy needs,
The untended unintended weeds,
Of gnarly ancestral seeds.

Unplowed acres of planted memories,
Soiled in fields of familial dreams,
Rooted in pastures old and muted.

Psychological legacies,
A past heritage of inherited versions,
Of a twisted truth,
Too tired to trust in truths unearthed,
Held steadfast in mature branches of family governance.
Buried before birth,
Deep within our consciousness.

We seek sanctuary in the nature of nostalgia's buxom breasts,
Nurturing mollycoddled lineage.
Resting our weary, teary souls
From the toils and spoils of childhood's past.

We harken back to bygone days,
Simpler times,
Crisp, clear, clarity.

Unshackle the protected falsehoods of the elders,

Tend the family tree,

Shower its core values with unfettered authenticity,

Betroth principled be-leaves with a luster not lacking in heritage or commonwealth.

The busy woodpecker barks out his triumphant melody.

A repetitious reminder,

To be kinder,

To our kindred, blinkered thinking.

The past pecking away at the presence...

Of the presents.

Resigning brothers and sisters,

To reflect on,

Neglect from,

The Mrs and Misters.

Histories branching out,

Keeping it real,

Based on pious bias "believe us if you try us" liars, THE LOT OF YA!

Long life preservers,

The undeserving,

Drowning in debt,

Protecting a lie they never met,

Projecting a lifetime's deep regret,

To cloud others, brothers, mothers, lovers,

Raking up the family's mysterious ways,

Invested in yesterday's real world passion plays.

We interpret reality with a bias which twists the available evidence according to a narrative that feels familiar,

but might be untrue,

To who we were and what we do,

Before we ever knew,

Of what and who,

Was actually there before us.

The ancestral anchor,

Should not weigh us down.

A past heritage of inherited versions,

Of a twisted truth.

Too tired to trust in truths unearthed,

Held steadfast in mature branches of family governance.

Buried before birth,

Deep within our consciousness.

Reality most bias.

letters from the heart

U

U R Me
I am U
4 us 2
R U
I O U
x

C, I x U
4 U + Me
= Us

O my x
U R DR 2 Me
So E Z on the I
R we in x
4 ever?
U & I

2 no Ps
Is 2 no U
2 no Y
Is 2 x

? not
2 no Y
Just B
U

4 UR only 4 Me

I O U

x

O K?

U 🔒'd ❤

U 🔍 the 🎁's

My ❤ takes ✈

I 🎧 in ur ⛪

⚓'d & ✉'d by u

U C Y?

⌚ our ✨'s collide

 In my I's

No U R 🔐

U R the 🔑

👂 Me

U R 'ed

U R Me

I am U

4 us 2

R U

I O U

x

C, I x U

4 U + Me

= Us

C

As you grow older, 'c' that you don't grow 'c'older

B

B 4 I ❤'d U

M T? No.

L OwN…

U R ❌LOwN

B C'N

B ❤'d

✅ in

❌BF's

♠ 8 the Zen z's

Z Q 2 B A:

is❌

R U M T

R U L OwN

Just B

& U R C'N

C U in U

B4 ❤ Oin

B C'N

B ❤'d

Just

B

Y

Judge not the Y

I C U in the emergent alpha-regrettable

B U

B4 A Y is answered back 2

4 U R OK

C, 3 P's R 2 B Q'd...

Patience?

Parlance?

Penance?

B live in the Y

Q will be answered

Peace will be found

But not in the Y

Judge not the Y

love

How Far

How far can we take this?
How far across the sprawling sea of hearts?
How long may we learn to live inside,
Outside the mind's eye.

How much may we learn,
Of waves splashing,
Crashing emotions,
Coloring our deep vistas,
Beyond what our imaginations joined possible,
Impossible frothy destinations,
Foaming at the water's edge,
The ledge where the land greets the sea,
Open mind, inside hearts,
Sandy love letters,
In-grains of soft sandy paths to adventures far,
Now how far,
At longest vast,
How far...

Neptune's plan is vast,
Behold the vast majesty,
Of past letters loved into grains of sand,
Swept away,
Never forgotten moments,
In time...
How far can we go?

Much left to learn?

Drowning willingly, into

Poseidon's powerful current,

Cupid's arrow all a-quiver,

Will deliver us from the depths of our sunken past,

Anchoring us to a new and safer harbor,

Deliverance of divine peace,

On the beaches of our hearts.

Love

LOVE... Leave - Only - Vital - Energy

SELF... Spiritual - Ever - Lasting - Freedom

LOVE 4 SELF = TRUTH

If the effort is equal the feelings will be mutualized

Truth = Consistency/Time

Dani ☺

Please embrace

The vulnerable space

Help me help you

Put a smile on your face.

Lack of Love

Lack of love for self inhibits compassion for others.

Lack of love for others suppresses self-esteem.

Digging

I'm digging the very thought of you...

Sifting amongst the shifting soul soil,
Scoping outside the plaintive panoply of self-regard,
Unearthing,
Mental-detecting,
Hardened-ground rules,
Softening bound-Aries.
I've found...

An introspective cerebral gold-rush,
Traversing down black-diamond-minds,
Flow-boarding half-piped notions,
Cascading mind moguls,
Of long quelled emotions,
Tending incendiary synapses.

Weaving brain juice smoothies into,
The incarcerated fibrous layered-cakes,
Baked of free-flowing emotion tumbles forth.

Defining moments,
Of meaningful movement toward,
Digging the very thought of you...

A Repetitive Recommissioning of memorial days,
Summing up the differences,
Total recall of what adds up,
Minus what didn't,
With effort equal,

Equating a mutually funded partnership

Of beauty-full,

Duty-full,

and free-quented,

Turns of events,

Cemented and spent,

Most heavenly sent.

The essential effervescent sensitivity of your essence,

I spy and clarify in my mind's eye,

Your candid incandescent presence,

To uncover the presents of your presence,

I'm digging the very thought of you...

You dig?

Make Living

Move beyond the numbers.

Quantify experiential data.

Accumulate memories.

Gain interest in life.

Invest in love.

Passion

Late morning respite from the leaves of last night's passion fall

Starry eyes and bleary eyed to it all

The unreal unfeeling nurture of love's nature

Reflected in the nomenclature of today's dirtied laundry

When emotions stir let the heart concur

19

The passionate flow of yesterday's stirrings

So let forth occurrings

Of a most delicate nature

Stays reflected in last night's hourglass of your mind

Seek and we may find

Passionate peace

Sweet release

Late evening respite from the cloud tears of my soul

For you...

For us all

Fight not the delicate nature of our dreams

Starry eyes and bleary to it all

Come one call all the passionate recall

Of my mind's recall

Of the industry of passion

Emotional fashion

In style

Out style

Smiles my heart

True love has a habit of returning.

Present

The gentle nature of your naive nurture

Is a gift,

Unwraps the emotional rift,

In the present.

The heart's desire on full display,

A will to stay,

Wrapped up in my emotional grey,

Is a present.

The love you share I feel,

I sense your need to heal,

Your presence raw and real,

You're a present.

Why

Why does a woman...

Why does a woman who longs for love sabotage it at the very moment of its inception?

Why does a woman who commits to truth in love break that commitment at the very moment she realizes it is within her grasp?

She is moved by it, feels it, senses it, hears it, feels it, believes it, experiences it in its purest most vulnerable essence and yet she runs from it... Why?

Does she not feel worthy of such a love?

Does she fear being seen for who she is?

Why is she so very frightened by its beauty that she runs from its presence?

Why does a woman retreat to isolation when she has yearned for companionship?

Why does she treat love like a battleground? The object of her affection in the cross hairs, transformed in her mind's eye to enemy status, annihilates it. Obliterates the love for its force is too overwhelming and omnipotent.

Why, in that moment of purity, does a woman FEEL the NEED to act against her own interests?

Why, when she has quested a lifetime to be loved and feel loved, and arrived at that moment, does she steal it from within her own grasp?

She does not BELIEVE in the feeling.

Scared from the past and scarred of the future when it's beholden...

Shutter Flutter

My heart was broken,
Alone and shuttered.
Then you came along,
And in love fluttered.

Simplicity

4:44 AM
Love is in the air
I sense it in your presence
I stroke it through your hair.

I see it in your eyes,
I feel it in your heart,
I hear it in your words,

Even when we are apart.

Grace,
Elegance,
Beauty,
True.
Life,
Love,
Trust,
You.

theories of the self

The Pain Equation

PAST x
+ Future Projections
 - Self Worth
 / Family
 = PAIN

The Truth Equation

Truth = Consistency/Time

The Shame Equation

Secrets + Silence + Judgment = Shame
Love = Empathy - Shame / Group
Privacy ✔ versus Secrets ✗

The Love Equation
I hear you - I'm sorry = Love

The Reality Equation

Seek equality in human beings; all being things equal.
When things don't add up, start subtracting in
= measure when hard times multiply.

Formulate opinions based on a division of the facts, non-plussed by irrational emoticons.

Feelings + truth - judgment/time = Reality

relationships

Revelationships

Eavesdrop on your heart and you could be spirited away to love,

Listen to the divine nurture of its natural rhythm and it may beat forever,

Bathe in the resultant revelationships

And happiness will adventure within you

Journeying to every nook of doubt,

Coursing through every crevice of fear,

Flowing into every fibrous tissue of your being human

To make you feel that which you were born to being - human.

Ride the ships of revelationships on the wave of love to the oceans of ecstasy.

Wife
by focal

Awake again,

Yet not alone,

Queen of my hearts,

Love on the throne.

What consumes the mind controls your life,

Future wife.

Folie à Deux

(A madness shared by two)

Filled up and fueled by her mother's failings,
Flailing upwards,
Spiraling down to unfeeling mediocrity,
Unaware of insobriety, in society,
She weaves,
Waving flags of attack dogs into the savage fray.

The acceptor - delusionary receptive,
The primary - elusively deceptive,
Repeating maladies old and new,
Of a madness shared by two.

Cunning stunts,
Symptomatically devious fronts,
Wants ordered by the General,
With needy, greedy expedient weaponry,
Housed in hollowed-out war chests,
Maladious melancholic reactionary action men,
Repeating maladies old and new,
Of a madness shared by two.

Deep Ending See 🔥

The discontentment
Of the unrelenting co-dependent,
Sum of her Hearts
Nurturing co-dependent parts,
Of her Dark (he)Arts
Adding fuel when her fire sparks,
Self-ignited, pain unrequited,
Emotional alighted, to a deeper ending see,
Blind to Co-Deep-Ending...See...

Holding on to lack of understanding,
Glad handing needs to feel connected,
Real, respected.
With friends she's disrespected,
Knowing not she's not protected,
From self-inflaming,
Naming and gaming, re-framing the truth,
Embedded from youth,
An uncouth shame sleuth,
Re-working, re-telling,
Like "Fuck-Its Cave Dwelling"
Rees-Cycle, Re-Selling.

Journey through the 🔥
Awaken desire,
Recovery to discovery,
Residing in Rees-sidual neurosis,
Not trusting or owning her own(ed) process.
Coco's distressed mess is hard to weave goodbye to.

Projecting and Infecting with lack of self-protecting of Mindscapes.
Safe, shallow waters
Mothers & Daughters,
Co-existing in a Deep-Ending-See.

She documents histories in 📝
Written JUDGMENTS
Self-Prescribed medicinal beliefs,
Imbibed griefs,
Chiefly set in her ways

A malaise of investing in the new ways,
Of feeling VERY,
InDoctrinated in Sperry,
Judging, begrudging in me,
Treading shallow waters, bathing free,
🏊 in a Deep-Ending See,
Of what shows & who knows blows.
Co-Deep Ending See.

The more I love in the face of projection
The less I respect her
The less she lessons herself
The more or less she respects me
The more I forgive her
The less she feels righteous
The less and the more
Mooring the lessons

The more I seek to accommodate her needs
The less accommodating she becomes
The more I return to love
The less she respects me
The less she listens to me
The more she hears nightmares
The more she loves herself
The less she loves me
Mooring the lessons

The more I accept her
The more she rejects me
The less I react
The more she acts out
The more I placate her
The less she respects me
The less I believe her
The more she loses faith in herself

Mooring the lessons

Woman

Hence when she woke,
Tortured, Alone,
Pining for the woods,
Reaching through branches overgrown snapping memory Owls of Knowing humanity.

Celestial mother,
See of my womb,
Flow nature's breath,
Unburden love's labor refound,
Re-imagining mindscapes of landfilled with love.
For love is the light,
Through darkness the path is clear,
The arable soil of my re-defined mind clean my iris.

Waft scriptures gently minded through the windows to my soul,
Spiriting me on Summer's resonant heart song,
For the Ocean of your love swims in my heart,
Stirs my Soul,
Enraptures my divinity,
A SEE of LoVe,
4 U R manifest Destiny.

Alive in your essence
Moist effervescence,
A countenance pure, undriven snow,
Crisp celestial moon glow,
Unclogging humanity in me,
4 2 C
I am alive.
Not for love, for land in love,
My urban myth hence departed,
Imparted truths imbued.

Man

Good natured man.
Of the kind of wo-man.

Man is fearless in sifting through his moral inventory,
Willing to surrender his version of the story.
Demystifying the mystery of his personal his-story,
Seeking inter-dependant glory.

Man, fall in love with self,
Sprinkle your joy dust on your own
memory shelf.

Man, warm hearted Man,
Nurturing the Mother Nature,
Deconstructing the nomenclature,
Of co-de-pen-dan-see
becoming In-de-pen-dan-sea
Man… Oh Man…

Best wishes Man.

Slipping

I feel us slipping
Dipping under the emotional waves
Drowning around
Closing the clown down
Drowsy
Lousy
Draining the ReesSources beside her
Pouring her time into anti-social-media distractions
Relationship 'pending'
Too busy me-friending
Lending and loaning
Bemoaning others
Making plans for Nigel
While Jonny makes plans

Define Grace

She said: "Loving the undeserving"
I said: "Simple Elegance"
Define your grace
Identify awakening
#Grace

The Soundtrack in my mind
The music of my maladies
The harmony of feelings
Symphonic self sympathy
My Epiphonic epitaph legacy
Meaning is ascribed subjective.
Nature is objective reality.

vulnerability

Wholesome of Heart

✗FULL of HOLES
✓SOME of WH♥LES

Feel whole in the heart and the truth is spoken,
If there's a hole in the heart, then the heart is broken,
Authenticity within emotional intimacy,
Lies within the terror of vulnerability.

Outward rage belies inward pain,
Rage by nature, shame by name.
Believing that which makes you vulnerable makes you beautiful is key,
Housed at the very core of understanding humanity.

Shame is the gatekeeper of an illusionary suspicion,
That the terror of vulnerability is an insurmountable condition.
The power of shame reflects this terror within,
And most folk know not where to begin.

To salvage love, imbue and impart,
Capture your rapture, be wholesome of heart.
Seek the vulnerable core of the shame in the self,
Dwell in its presence, reside in its wealth.

Vulnerability is at the core of shame all above,
For it is also the birthplace of authentic love.
Vulnerability is at the core of shame all above,
For it is also the birthplace, of authentic love.

(Un)Broken

Broken, unspoken, mixed up messages
Last vestiges of hope sunk,
Love drunk and broken.

Board up the heart shutters,
Bruised in the stagnant morning gutters,
Laid bare, truth awoken,
Love sick and broken.

I will not run, even though you chase me away,
I will not hide, even though you ignore the truth,
I will not fear feelings left in the unspoken,
My love is strong,
Lasts long,
I know in my heart of hearts where I belong...
Unbroken

Breathing Out

Hollow chested,
Open harm's way,
Days end recalls recoiled events along the way.

Closed off,
Feelings too painful,
Change is pain…pain is changeful.

Arms wide open,
Eyes shut wide,
Ride the waves inside outside.

People

Courageous people persevere.
Kind people understand.
Compassionate people accept.
Strong people forgive.
Intelligent people ignore.
Weak people revenge.
Successful people endow.
Connected people thrive.
Mature people keep growing.
Vulnerable people love

A Poem

A poem shared is a truth dared... a soul bared.

Going to pieces without falling apart

Going to pieces without falling apart,
Holding your ground when the rug's pulled from under you,
Soaring to new heights when your wings have been clipped.

Cave

My tits won't behave
My bits need a shave
If I carry on like this I'll end up in an early grave
I think I need my cave.

Vulnerhate

Invulnerably, mankind rages against its own mind machine.

Avoiding the Issues

Constantly seeking issues
Avoiding the real ones.

The Emotional Penitentiary

She resides in her own mind,
Dismembering memories of self,
Upon her memory shelf.

Reeling,
From feeling,
Desperately unable to answer the what's and why's,
Unable to disguise,
That sparkle in her eyes,
A vision of temporary relief,
From the unstoppable grief,
of the Emotional Penitentiary.

Seeking out the seemingly unfindable answers,
Not found from losers or chancers,
Or the tiniest of dancers.
Criminal Minds committing to fitting,
Diagnosis of mental health,
Invested from someone else's emotional wealth.
Stealth bombers,
Carpeting the halls of mess,
With no redress,
No physical address,
For the living stress,
Locked away…
In the Emotional Penitentiary.

Imma-traumaty

Understanding shame,
Without the need for self-blame,
Pockets of toxic baggage,
Carried in over-packed excess,
Cast in-visible shadows,
Soothing strains of empathetic connection,
The intersection of imma-traumaty,
Social non-conformity.

Secret, Silent, Judgment,
+ blame
= Shame

Mid-life crisis is the psyche's desire to reconnect with the soul of emotion dormantly trapped in the child spirit by the risen ego of the traumatized adult

addiction

The 13th Step

The 13th Step is an Emotional Amendment to the Spiritual Bill of Rights that is the first 12.

13th Step Manifesto

Feeling our friends
Words in our bond
(En)Lightning the hearts way
To break through beyond

Soldier of Sobriety

Personal attacks,
From the oversized ego in the green shirt,
Black and white opinions held firm,
In grey-haired slicked back maladies,
Non-melodic and dramatically-mellow,
Yellow-crested story-teller,
Incarcerated brain-dweller.

Billing himself and everyone around,
Stunningly stubborn insubordination.
Fourteen days of holding on,
Soldier of Sobriety,
Regimented impropriety,
Ritualistic in a narcissistic venue,
Corny beefed, re-hashed dishes from his karmic menu.

Covering up the cracks,
With personal attacks,
Working the social in the group,
Like a girl scout troop.

Opinions long fermented,
Cemented,
Regimented,
Staving off the brain indented,
Less frequented,
More demented.

Delicious maliciousness,
Abrupt eruptions,
Diminishing returns,
Lessons unlearned,
Personal attacks,
By the soldier of sobriety,
Whose deity is less than best,
Invested in distrust best left in his war chest.

The Judge-mental Judge-meant in mental states,
His splitting of the most greyest of hairs,
A stilted, wilted, stoic state of affairs,
Of who-ifs and what-cares,
Entailed in the old-fangled slicked back rhetorical follicles,
Of his judge-mental slicked back entrenched grey-hairs.

Feeling,
Emotionally drunk,
Sober from vulnerability,
Incalculable culpability,

Inflexible,

Cyclical,

Round and round he goes,

Spiraling down,

His singular brain muscle, he'll flex it,

De-valuing his personal currency post Brexit,

Repeating repetitive miss-steps,

Orders,

Banded about,

Handed out,

By General Notoriety,

Ingrained in the old-fangled slicked grey haired rhetorical follicles,

Of The Soldier of Sobriety.

The Gift

The guilt is not the same

As the shame that is to blame

For the rages of the ages

Comes and goes at different stages

To rid it from society

Authenticity is required see

For emotional sobrie-ty

To be garnished and accepted

Fore shame makes it so rejected

Mirror self, be self-reflected

And protected from projected altered

States of mind neglected

To attain a higher status

Let not the denigrates berate us

For authenticity is key

If we form consistency

Consistently

Striving for sober living

Safe from all miss-giving

Toxic past forgiving

Carried shame re-living

Be true

To you

And only you

For most times we know not what we do

We try to hear but misconstrue

Our values skew

Ragers, shamers

Guilters, blamers

Pain inflamers

Live, love, forgive? Forget

Accept pain, Reject regret

Stall all negativity

And just be

Just be

The you you never knew

who to be

before you grew

Reflected on the self

Self-wealth not material

Ethereal and believable

By all accounts receivable

The guilt is not the same

As the shame that is to blame

Tis the reason for the treason

Ebbs and flows within the season

Offers neither rhyme nor reason

For the rages of the ages

Comes and goes at different stages
To rid it from society
Authenticity is required see
For emotional sobriety
That is key
The key
I've gifted me

The Game

Humans...

Turn to their addictions when the pain is too intense,
Common childhood trauma all too common, makes no common sense.

That trauma left the station with a lack of introspection,
Self-collision imminent with shards of self-reflection,
The childhood ego crucified, parents on the cross,
Existential crisis causes suffering and loss.

Toxic shame is carried and the child is not protected,
Then adult debt is realized and shame and pain projected,
The self is disrespected,
Till history's inspected.

Doctors told that medicine is not too much addictive,
Taught by institutions, don't be oxo-narc-restrictive,
This new drug that we're pushing relieves all their hurt and pain,
Makes us many millions, their suffering, our gain.

Push this OxyContin for the patients in your care,
Then concentrate it stronger, get the people on a tear.
Big profits for big pharma causes misery for you,

Government's unhappy, so what's a Fed to do?

Crack down on illicit use - make it harder to procure,

Replace the space with heroine, the new drug in the store.

Addicts to the clinics, insurance pays the cost,

A temporary band aid - a generation lost.

Wandering, blundering

Squandering, wondering,

Who will question forcefully this social impropriety,

And talk of truth, real cure for youth - 'emotional sobriety'

Addiction's not a disease,

It's a symptom... please

Understand this.

Humans...

...turn to their addictions when the pain is too intense,

And though I am no expert, I have much ex-pe-rience.

Challenging a long held belief

Can sometimes bring about lasting relief.

Pharma says 'addiction is disease' for a reason,

So health insurance covers treatment, mo-ne-ta-ry treason,

Then repeat the cycle to regurgitate the dough,

A manufactured crisis so the money stream don't slow

Grease up the fiscal flow

We're paying blow by blow,

for blow

after blow.

"Let's earmark fiscal spending,

for solutions, let's not fudge-it,
Create new sub-committees,
Work the numbers in the budget,
Clinics, pamphlets, meetings, plans, the answers what we learn ya,"
A scary moral high ground,
A terror-sorta-firma

The vexing,
Perplexing notion of,
Infection of a hexing lotion,
Devotion to the commotion of injecting the heroine potion,

Rejection of the
Heroines and heroes
In the Emperor's clothes,
Yesterday's Nero's to overnight zeroes
Numb the pain,
Locate the vein,
Escape the game.

The Billy-Bob's & Betty Sue's,
For years been paying Mountain Dew's,
Paying through their teeth.

The priestly husbands, nuns and tarts,
Blow Charlie up their body parts,
Paying through their noses.
Still… the garden smells of roses.
Until recently…

Shit's been fucked up for years,
America did not shed any tears.
Until recently…

43

Urban didn't matter, just incarcerate the blacks,

But now the war on drugs moved to the white side of the tracks,

Middle class Caucasian, a picture that's disturbin'

So-ciety got pious when addiction went sub-urban

See now the epidemic ain't restricted to the 'thugs'

The 'projects' spread to neighborhoods not used to wars on drugs,

The neatly tailored gardens and the whitest picket fences,

Are fragile fickle front-lines of sub-urban-ite defenses.

The menace is,

For the Marjorie's & Dennis's,

The boundary line's been broken.

They now live in very changing times,

With real time shifting border lines.

A new project for the white projects,

To project their shame and blame,

No longer able to escape 'The Game'

They're now a part of 'The Game.'

Feeling the pain and the shame and the brain drain of life in 'The Game.'

Unsobering reality,

Abnormal in its normal-see

Humans...

...turn to their addictions when the pain is all too real

Gambling, drugs, sex, alcohol will stop the addict feel,

But pain is what we need to face, is what we need to cure,

A real and lasting remedy, not found in a drug store

Our ills

Cannot be cured in any lasting way by pills,

Or rehabilitation centers, that center on the surface and not at the heart

of the matter,

That's what's the matter with our system,
So many issues, it's painful to list-em,
No shock that we missed-em.

The 'experts' say the 'symptom' is the problem, the 'disease'
"Addiction's the affliction, take these 12 steps if you please."
Betty down @ Castle Ford, cannot afford to trade in truth,
In real and lasting cure for youth,
She must repeat the cycle so,
She treats the surface, s'all a show,
She needs 'em to keep coming back,
To keep the cash cow in the black,
Milky white lies - ain't no surprise,
Addiction rates are on the rise,
Dollar signs in Betty's eyes,
@ Castle Ford, she can't afford,
To get to the root of The Game,
She's a ruler by nature and name,
Trades in symptoms and surface and shame...

Oh well
All's well that ends

My friends...
what if...

We dare to dream,
And we choose to craft and weave it,
A future so fantastic that it's hard to make believe it,
But let's try to make it real,
To simply share with humanity exactly how we feel,
Authentically,
Consistently,

45

Consistent authenticity,
Make truth our new reality.

Reverse the social networks' way of thinking,
Strive to come alive and get our Tweeting FaceBooks Linkedin.
Prevent ourselves, from presenting ourselves,
As the best version we invent of ourselves.

what if…

One day
We switch off
E-lec-tronic-lAy
Instead plug in to feelings, so
That we could share our feelings, WHOA!
A fucking scary concept bro

what if...

What we tweet and 'share' and say,
Is how we REALLY feel?
I guaran-fuckin-tee it that would keep it fuckin real.
"I'm confused, I'm angry, I'm conflicted, I'm heartbroken"
Society connected cause the truth's at last been spoken?
"I feel alone, I feel depressed, I didn't know you cared"
Society connected cause the truth's at last been shared,
Our feelings all been bared,
Our voices all been heard.

Let's work for that cause,
not for applause.
Live life to express,
not to impress.

Be less about self,

Self-less.

Humility is not thinking less of yourself,

It's thinking of yourself less…ness.

My God bless our blessed dominion,

Changed by example and not by opinion.

Humans…

All feel pain,

We all know shame,

We all bleed the same,

So let us ALL dare to change the rules and the rulers of 'The Game.'

spirit

Hear - See - Feel

The words "I hear you" will stop people dead in the negative track they are on & make them feel very much alive.

The words "I see you" will unblinker the overthinker, instantly illuminating a path to a state of enlightened affairs.

The words "I feel you" will connect empty vessels to a kindred spirituality that will flow and fill the hearts and minds of man's-kindness.

Musing

An example of good character is to embrace unpleasant characters with civility.

A test of humility is to willingly retreat from deserved adulation.

A sense of serenity garners contempt for hubris.

A lie withheld has already been found out within.

And conduct becoming a gentle man engenders melodious civility - the antitheses of an orchestrated event produces ethical harmony.

Work for (pursue) knowledge, devote to feeling emotion (a sense of God), energize purpose (inner 7 chakras).

Inflect Intellect, infiltrate (your owned) karma.

Listen to your karma talk with you.

Pursue emotional aspirated devotion to energize knowledged enlightenment.

Still Here

The lyrical tabloid sleaze you trade in daily,
Will not sway me.

Vocalized, localized venting over venti coffee,
Will not grind me down.

The twitching, mouse-itching jerkings of your out-ternet anti-socialist networkings,
Will not disconnect me.

The muted shrill of pillow talk under the whispered cover up of your bordello novello,
Will not characterize me.

In spite of your worst intentions
I'm still here.

Begin Again

When you get to the end of all that you know,
And your journey is questioned within,
Reach deep down inside of all that you know,
Then your journey of life may begin.

Grandfather 🌙

Grandfather moon,
Connection to the stars,
Fill my heart with glow,
So that I may flow,
And be known,
Know,
And 🐝,
Known.

In-to-MaTely,
Orbit within my atmosphere.

🌙 Rays,
Stretch your reach,
Bridge your Glow,
The morning Songbird will know,
Will see,
Will feel,
Sings of your divinity quest,
The Robin wears it best,
Nested, crested, proud breasted,
For all humaniTree,
To feel Mother's Earth,
A reborn morning glory story.

Old Father Moon

Old Father Moon,

Watcher of the night.

Illuminate our consciousness with divine naivety.

Bless the minds and hearts of children of the world with deities of joy and oft lost innocence while they more peaceful slumber half circle round this mortal coil.

Mother Sun radiates.

Father Moon the stronghold of the common sense.

Awakening the spirit within the kindred commonwealth of man's kind humanities to tether, fuse, and anchor Mother's love.

Religion is for people who are afraid of going to hell
Spirituality is for people who have already been there
Humanity should be our race. Love our religion.

Spirit World

Populate your world with objects of beauty,
Quality that delights the soul and electrifies the spirit.

The Iris of the Mind's eye

See through the iris of the mind's eye.
Take shots at life,
Don't just point and shoot,
Take a beat to focus on what matters.

Develop from the negatives,
Nurture the courage to expose yourself to vulnerability,
Capture the positives.

Hidden signs of life may be revealed,
If you illuminate the iris in the mind's eye.
If things don't frame out well,

Re-focus and take another shot.

Steady Your Mile-age

Steady your mile-age,

Constant.

Journey one step at a time,

A journey of a thousand miles does begin with one step, but a thousand steps in the same spot is not a journey and will get you nowhere fast.

Present

Unwrap the gift of the present,

Free from the confines of our yester-morrows,

Each-moment-only-once.

Zen

Now and zen

I wish upon but then

Realize I'm now longer zen

When I gave up…

When I gave up the fight to be someone else's hero, I was able to save myself.

When I gave up looking for a spiritual connection I found one.

Path

Give gratitude,
take not pleasure away from others.

Lift your own spirits,
and others will be spirited away with you.

Allow another to drag you down,
and all manner of yestermorrows will haunt your todays.

Your path will become clear only when you look into your heart.
Investigate your soul.
Who looks outside, dreams.
Who looks inside, awakens.

The Bright Light

The brightest light,
Glows in spite of,
Blows in light of.

Flow

Once arrived at, let it go,
Memorize the feelings, then let go the flow.

Desire

When you get what you desire
and you're not prepared to nurture it
Desire will desert you
You will get what you deserved,
and lose what you desired.

Alive

It's not the load that breaks you down. It's the way you carry it.
It's not life that makes you feel alive. It's how you live it.
It's not the love that lifts you up. It's your capacity to share it.

Carry the burden.
Live your life.
Share the love.

Humanity

If we are unable to accept our mortality, we avoid living in the moment.
If we are unable to believe in our humanity, we seek God in others or act God-like ourselves.

My Path

Follow the signs wherever they lead, seek them out, notice them - road, music, texts, telephone, new human encounters. Let go

Let go of control and embrace the signs in your core. Listen to people with curiosity.

Remain connected to God and spirituality.

Hear the shamanic conversations during word exchanges and the power over yourself this affords. This understanding and experiencing on a daily basis will prove liberating and educational, and brilliantly insightfully interesting.

Marvel at the awesome power of shame and how understanding it frees your spirit to fly higher, to achieve heights never dreamed of.

People❀Things

People were created to be loved.

Things were created to be used.

The reason why the world is in chaos is because things are being loved and people are being used.

Imperical Spherical

The Imperical Spherical Numerical Indus-Tree-Us in all of EYE

When the Spirit Leaves the Body

When the Spirit Leaves the Body
The SPIRIT FALLS to the Earth

Sense

The earthly sense is the ladder to the universe,
The religious sense is the gateway to Heaven,
The spiritual sense is the bridge to the emotional World.

Tree-Mends-Us

The mind bending splendorous truncated satiated seed,
Befriends us,
Lends us back a part of the wholeness,
Divine refinement,
Nietzsche's rejection of religious inspection,
Reminds the kind in mankind,
Of an outward perception,
Found within,
Nestling in the conception,
Birthed introspection,
The immaculate pre-conceived perception
The earth can mend us,
Feels tree-mend-us
Transcends us.

Resident solemnity,
Of the chi that lives outside the mystery of me.

Current electrical focus,
Seeks to prod and hocus-poke-us,
Reminds us what first awoke us,
To awaken what was taken…
Seek out the lost child,
Re-cycle the earth,

Re-kindle the spark extinguished at birth.

These uncommon times are nature's superlative gifts,

Healing tears and rifts,

Supernatural geographical visions,

Born of deliberate decisive decisions,

To see

And be seen

Love and be loved.

Magnolia, branches wide,

Resides outside, across the street,

Two tall Palms,

A handy reminder of religious psalms,

Calms the way, out of harming,

Disarming the constructed, instructed self of who we became...expected ourselves to be...

To be free... again

Return to me... again

A rebirth of the me,

A need to reseed,

I planted my seed in view of three...

The earth can mend us,

Feels tree-mend-us

Transcends us.

In the Garden

Listen to the birdsong,
See the joy it makes,
I tend to, keep my grass cut,
So that I can see the snakes.

Nurturing the hedge-rows,
With a natural demeanor.
I'm too busy tending my grass,
To see if yours is greener.

In the Garden...
Pollinate the landscape,
Trim the (h)edges, bed in, harden,
In the Garden.

There is Longing

There is longing... Longing to love and learning to be loved
Yearning to leave the past... Learning to pass the yearning
Hearing the needs of now... Knowing the now is all we have left behind us
Trusting the uncertain future projections
Faith in self - Love thy self
Selflessness - Soulfulness - Residing in the shadows of sunlight
Combining loves in life's lived
Supporting the found knowledge of creation of a new... Knewing the now
Grieving past resentments - Wo(manifesting) fresh hope
Fertilizing + surprising the current landscape with seeds of shared abundance
The impeccability of thought
Mindsfull of singular commonality

Thrusting the trust

Knowing the nowness is all we have needed

To belong

To another

2 each other

To ourselves

Shut Eye

Time for shut eye

Rest the mind

Bless the body

Sleeping blind

Phoenix Flames

The smoldering embers,

of Boy Scout bonfires,

Laid bare in Phoenix,

Risen from deserted flames.

Illuminating the dark shadows,

of expected wrong doings,

Recycling the ashes,

Encrusted in the dust.

Needs want,

Bleeds must.

In self we doubt,

In spite we trust.

Laid bare in Phoenix,
Risen from deserted flames,
The smoldering embers,
of Boy Scout bonfires.

The Invisible Tree

Ah humanity
The invisible tree
The barrier to humani-tree
Scorched in the parched earth right in behind me
Wistful Windows to the distant yonder
Branching out your green collage
Under a canopy of indus-tree
Smokey plumes of Mrs. 1950.

Obscene to be Heard

Should we traverse this mortal coil,
Powered by the rhapsodic wonder of wind?
Amped up by the solo solar-power of eclectic electrical trickling currents of wonderment.
Or the slick efficiency of oil?

Delving deep into the rich, cavernous complexities of industrial restitution and fatalistic individualistic absolution,
Titans of industry must be obscene to be heard.

Divinical retribution.

Forgive the squinting rapscallion his miscreant nature,
Until he crudely pollutes the sea of our humanities,
with the oily slick bottled up forgotten love notes to self,
that feel better off dread and very much a-lie.

61

Mr. Oily McSlick, sell me another tabloid glory-hole,
Lose me in the morning story of your board rooms of boredom.

Make me pine for that fresh I wanted but never didn't need nor make sense of.
My propensity,
For something a lot less shallow,
And little more density.

Oozy smarming, charmless alarming,
Currying flavor with Prince Charming of shameful greed.
Confusing wants with breed-ing,
Needs with convoluted unheralded un-heeding,
Bleeding from the un-corporational wounds re-seeding.

Sub-verse, re-abuse, re-cyclone,
Now is the Winterfell of our discontent.

Supplant then recede back into the arrested 'TIMBEEER' of the forest foliage of
Uncamoflaged inequitable futures,
A mutual-fund of inequality,
A pensioner's unrealized allowance of a frostbitten 'sea-I-told-you-so' of hope.

Paralyze the petroleum seagull of my blind man's bluff,
On the beach of shame-fueled industrial restitution.,
Out of reach from lame brains,
Drained by a needier, ever-greedier media.

Nature will go public on your greasy exchange of stock Mr. Oily McSlick.
You greasy naive globule of inhumanity,
Epitomizing vanity,
Trading in sanity,

You dirty, gooey, greasy oily pin-prick.

Should we traverse this mortal coil,

Powered by the rhapsodic wonder of wind?

Amped up by the solo solar-power of eclectic electrical trickling currents of wonderment.

Or the slick efficiency of oil?

Delving deep into the rich, cavernous complexities of industrial restitution and fatalistic individualistic absolution,

Titans of industry must be obscene to be heard.

Hero

Heroes come in many different shapes and sizes

Wearing a myriad of masks and multiple (dis)guises.

Two TREES

Two TREES shall not Enter+Twine

Nowness

I have no time like the present

To reach into the moon

Disappear into the stars

Search into the soul of mankind

Feel the human spirit

Fraud Squad

You'll never make it if you fake it till you make it
Authenticate the spark
Ignite consistent truth
Define your grace in humble space

Fake it till you make it gives arrival to pretense,
Accepted common sense, successes last defense
Forming your own fraud squad will imposterize your senses,
Making it and faking it builds only false pretenses.

2nd Nature

Oh what a tangled world wide web we weave,
When first we practice presenting ourselves,
As the best version we invent of ourselves,
To feel content with ourselves,
So that we may circumvent our true nature,
Of wheeling and dealing within our feeling.

Living in the spin,
Caught up in the attractions,
Of the net-inter-actives and gross-inter-actions.
This patterned looped behavior is learned,
Ingrained, burned.
It becomes '2nd nature'

Now the nature of the primal 1st desires - self-revelation of authentic truths real feelings of love.

Are relegated to a place behind the needs of the dominant '2nd nature' - public appearance of inauthentic belies experiences of pain.

truth

Dishonorable Judgment

Dishonorable judgment and self-righteous indignation will enslave a person in contempt of themselves.

Grave Matters

All judgments passed on others,

Belong in the court of self-opinion,

Take not a part of the blame,

Accept not projections of shame.

Blame past to others,

Is judgment passed on self,

To begin a sentence of revenge…

Dig Two Graves.

Reputable Appearance

The worst way to lose a bad reputation is to endeavor to be what appears desirable.

The best way to gain a good reputation is to endeavor to be what you desire to appear.

Luster

We are drowning in information,

While starving for wisdom.

Climbing mountains,

While making mole-hills.

Scarred from birth,

Afraid to live,

Scared to death.

Life after death,
Love before death.

We are drowning in information,
While starving for wisdom.
Overcoming mountains,
While making mole-hills.

We are scarred at birth,
Afraid to live,
Scared to death.

Life is the present,
Release the fear,
Embrace the pain,
Feel alive,
Love before death.

The Crow

The Crow must learn to work
The Wolf must learn to floW
The Crow & Wolf must learn to work together

The Crow learns to work
The Wolf learns to floW
The Crow & Wolf learn to work together

The CROW learns how to WORC in the WOLF FLOW
The WOLF learns how to FLOW in the CROW WORC
WORC with the WOLF
FLOW with the CROW

Fight against fighting for your rights

You trample on my rights,

Espousing wrongs.

You project and infect,

Your childhood neglect,

What's left of MY rights?

Pain is not your exclusive domain,

Your stinging refrain,

For emotional gain,

Will drain our love.

Dispose of your emotional garbage again and again.

I won't complain.

My right to sit with my pain and be with that little boy again...and again.

True

Pain disguised as anger,

Masking anguish disguised as rage.

Turn the page,

Don't fight the feelings.

It's no use not knowing the painful truth.

Calm

The calm after the storm
The birth after re-born,
The dew inside the dawn,
I'm fond,
Of the charm of James Bond,
But prefer weathered and worn.
The stealth in Jason Bourne.

No self-harm,
No cause for alarm,
Farm out the calm,
JB's got your back,
When the flack fires back,
Cometh the man, Cometh the hour,
I marvel,
At the power of Jack Bauer,
But prefer weathered and worn,
The complex in Jason Bourne.
The dew inside the dawn,
The calm after the storm
The birth after the porn,
The stealth in Jason Re-Bourne.

4 kin A

A state of recovery
A joy in discovery
A truth unbound
A lost love found

In One Moment

In one moment life can be forever changed,
One choice lie can devastate a lifetime.
Fortified Kingdoms crushed by she who shared the throne.
Thorny crowns ripped and torn from the King's head.

His Majesty will ride again,
Not so parading in gilded carriages,
He will be led to a new throne,
Not so echoing footsteps through marbled palatial corridors.

The King will place a new crown on his stately mind.
His Queen will know of treachery,
and rid it from the Kingdom.
Before she sits with the King,
He will have shown mercy within his realm.

The Royal Subject shall be divinity,
A Plantagenet dynasty less invested in tyrants,
The family crest presenting no harm nor heritage lost,
In one moment life can be forever changed.

Judge

Victory is meaningless if you're fighting the wrong battle,
Justice will not be served until those who are unaffected are as upset as those who are.
To see that the world doesn't judge you, stop judging yourself.
You will always receive justice in the court of self-righteous.

Pigment

The pigmentation of our skin is not a barometer of social status,

It must never preclude civility, fairness and equality within our society, or future generations will hate us for it,

Or against it?

There's no in between,

Switzerland does not reside in the extreme.

Everything's not all White.

Currently the currency is inate begrudgemnt,

Labelling another based on hate and judgment,

The haves, and the have nots,

Tied up in relational knots,

Enslaved in chains,

Enraged in Watts,

'It's all white' is the chitter-chatter,

We all know that black lives matter,

Splatter the black matter of the value of life,

Far and wide,

Across social media's divide

The pigmentation of our skin is not a barometer of social status,

It must never preclude civility, fairness and equality within our society, or future generations will hate us for it,

Or against it?

How thick is your skin?

Heard

Negate the need for negativity,

Cleanse the sub-conscious conscripts of our mind-less-ness,

Do the dance of circumstance,

Remove the fog of pessi-mist,

Re-fine the sublime center,

Re-wire the fantastical elastical strands of our marching mind bands,

Fashion a free-style of compassion,

Actions speak louder than words,

So believe what you see,

And fuck what you Heard

(amber)

Flow

Once arrived at, let it go,

Memorize the feelings, then let go the flow.

Lying In

In silky pajamas she lay,

The lady of superficial meaning,

Ingesting in resting,

Investing in yesterday's stock price,

The blue-vested nested trader,

Dropped twice,

A nicer DarthVader.

Since the brexit exit of

Island nations deviations.

Setting in stone cold blue,

Truths abused,

Colonizing xenophobic fears,

Over decaying years

Tears for fears

The needs of everybody's wants to rule the world.

Bedded in.

Crying.

Lying in.

The Good - The Bad

Respiration (Pete Rock remix)

The good, the bad, the black the white,

The love and the hate, the struggle and the fight,

The Ku Klux Clan and the far far white,

The left of center and the right.

In order to extrapolate the lies from the fiction,

We need to find a common ground, avoiding contradiction,

But diction is required when the truth's unpacked,

Clarity's synonymous to fact.

The world's gone crazy, societies lazy,

The outlook's bleak and the future's hazy.

Gun's got bigger, more happy on the trigger,

Po-lice fearful, shoot another black man,

Take your rights back man, pick up the slack,

Kill another cop, put a bullet in the back.

Chitter, chatter, praise, flatter,

Blood, splatter, life, tatter,

The truth and the lies of the former and the latter,

All lives matter is the fact of the matter.

72

The good, the bad, the black the white,
The love and the hate, the struggle and the fight,
The Ku Klux Clan and the far far white,
The left of center and the right.

Guns and muscle and brawn no brain,
"You stole my fucking country - flushed it down the drain!"
Stealing my America, liberal motherfucker,
Shove yer bleeding heart, I ain't no fucking sucker,
We hear you loud and clear (Woo-Hoo!)
We hear your right wing cheer (Fuck You)
We hear you, cheer you, "Love Trumps Palin"
No-one said the passageway to Plymouth's plain sailing…

Cometh the man, cometh the hour,
Cometh the pilgrim in the May-Mayflower.
Cometh the shiny silver buckles on the shoes,
The red of America bled white, blues.

The good, the bad, the black the white,
The love and the hate, the struggle and the fight,
The Ku Klux Clan and the far far white,
The left of center and the right.

The pilgrims sailed from England to escape religious pains,
A new frontier was spreading west to realize the gains,
The tomahawks of freedom met with Remingtons to brains,
Colonize America with Africans in chains.
Steal 'em from their families, devoid of any hope,
Shoot 'em up with dope, and hope they stay afloat.
Amis-mother, Amis-sister, Amis-brother, Amis-dad,
The whites went dark and world went mad.

The good, the bad, the black the white,

The love and the hate, the struggle and the fight,

The Ku Klux Clan and the far far white,

The left of center and the right.

Purification of the man,

Implementation of the plan,

The uptight, extreme, right wing clan.

They always mess it up,

Always dress it up.

Clinging to divinity, they always bless it up.

The deep south chapter, right wing curse,

Preaching hatred, chapter & verse.

Claiming white supremacy while dressing like a clown,

They show us how to dress it up but how they gonna live it down.

The good, the bad, the black the white,

The love and the hate, the struggle and the fight,

The Ku Klux Clan and the far far white,

The left of center and the right.

But how to conquer shame, set aside the blame,

Struggle with the notion that we all ain't born the same.

Our birth rights differ, we come from different places,

Judged on spec by the pigment in our faces.

(slow down)

The current White House Resident,

Happens to be, the first black President, (two-term)

Dignity and brains, no brawn,

Walks the black on the White House lawn.

The fear of Farrakhan, the hate of Bill O'Reilly

The right can't hear you Tavis, even though you're Smiley.

They barrack Barack, he fights rights black,

With erudite civility, the truth is still on track.

Wise up, size up the lies before our eyes, tear up

Clear up untruths, no surprise,

Anger in the eyes, addictions on the rise,

The poor less ignorant, the rich less wise.

The tight knit po-lice tightly wound.

Judge him on the spot, just get him on the ground.

It used to be the birch, now it's stop and search,

Ask questions later, just cuff the fucker first.

Throw him in a cell, let him go to hell,

Knock him out for life, until they toll the final bell.

Riots on the streets, looting of the bling-dom,

The OJ Queen in the Rodney King-dom.

The good, the bad, the black the white,

The love and the hate, the struggle and the fight,

The Ku Klux Clan and the far far white,

The left of center and the right.

Politics on fire, feeling the Bern-ie,

"Don't stop believing'" we're all on the Journey,

With 'Open Arms', and closed email accounts,

We put our faith in the Hillary in varying amounts,

The only other option is Donald the Duck,

He could become the Chief unless we start to give a flying fuck?

Trumped up charges, fears on sale,

Look who's at the checkout, the white's beyond the pale.

The good, the bad, the black the white,
The love and the hate, the struggle and the fight,
The Ku Klux Clan and the far far white,
The left of center and the right.
The good, the bad, the black the white,
The love and the hate, the struggle and the fight,
The Ku Klux Clan and the far far white,
The left of center and the right.

And the right.
And the right.
And the right.

Being Porn

The trouble
With being porn
Is that Internet born
Makes you feel dirty
In the Inter-wet morn

Plucking Joking

You're plucking joking,
Porous re-harmer,
Facial Dalai-Lama,
Eyelid Karma for aesthetic nirvana,
The esthetician magician,
Waxing the lyrical extractions,
Of painted deities,
Most wrinkled frailties.

Oily goopy globules of face medicine,
Derivations of treatments meant to expose
And cover up, from eye to nose
Life's brutal blows.

Hide the Gremlins from the "Bright-Light,"
Porous pock marks in plainest sight,
Indivisible to one facial nation under God.

A sight for more eyes,
Strips of cotton neatly placed on faces,
Masking and tracing the miss-placed lost graces of our past disgraces.

The 'Clean the Dream' factory,
Detracting the refracted lenses in the spectacle of strangers,
Weigh-Lated in the mangers of belated baby ladies,
Questing youth's fountainous lie,
Fleetingly cheating nature's eventual catch,
Highbrow notions of eye-brow lotions,
To blot out the natural signs of aging,
Fully graced by full faced beauty fucking,
Orgasmic face poking,
You're plucking joking?

You Done Good

You done good,
New you would,
Sin your blood.

Bath

She takes a bath most every night
The lady of the shadow bright
Shining darkness
Hidden truth
Fear for-saken
In her youth

Cleansing and cleaning
Redeeming her dirty
Perdy
Okie folksy liquid redux remedy

No hub-bub
In the tub-of
Smokey hollowed love.

Rinse clean the abandoned truck stop hair extenstion-cropted
Once abandoned
Twice adopted
By Father Time and I
Lucifer's antidote rids the affliction
Her predilection

For her addiction

Is rinsed clear and clean most every night

The lady of the shadows bright

She takes a bath most every night

4

When 1 is 2 non-plussed
4 just isn't fussed

The inner significance of perceived sensory inertia through time and space.

The Phenomenology of the Human Cosmic Torpedo.

The tangential experience of inner significance as perceived sensory inertia personified in free fall, re-defines gravity senses and enraptures the sub-cranial nerve stem, stimulating a nexus of euphoric moments through time and space. A neural limbic nirvana in the sky-realm.

Pull the chord to stabilize and re-gravitate the weight of the atmospheric pressure of humanity magnetizing you back to 🌓

soul

Echo Retreat Repeat

Echo Retreat Repeat
Snap judgments bend integrity stretching the truth breaking integrity,
Suspending disbelief.

Tighten unquestioned beliefs constructing walls defending principles unfounded,
Gravity less grounded.

Controlled environments restrict access to unsafe primal instinct,
Analysis paralysis.

Interest vested chaos manifests insecure surface investment maturation,
Procrastination deficit disorder.

Factor out redundant material behavior related to stagnant imperious nostalgia,
Manhandled old-fangled flights of fancy.
Love's labour lusted after,
Life's labors lost.

Before scores of frosty costly crusades engage weary foes losing crusades,
Plunder neural fortitude regarding damage of the collateral kind.
Surrendering memorial wakes confined.
Echo. Retreat. Repeat.

The Calamity of Conscience

The cerebral paradox
The illusive obvious
The letting go of holding on
Finding by not looking
Unearthing without disturbing the ground.
Going to pieces without falling apart.
Accepting answers without question.
Unconscious incompetence
Conscious incompetence
Conscious competence
Unconscious competence

Loosen Lucidity

Loosen lucidity
Emotional liquidity
Permission to feel
Connection to real
Truth spoken
Spirit woken
Alive
Thrive
Loosen lucidity.

Gentle Mind

Arrest the mind, detain the thinking,
Save the wounded child from sinking.
Unpack the cruel, release the kind,
Be still in body, gentle mind.

Hate the timid in-timid haters,
Self-intervention of cyclic natures.
Grading the no-man's land of my psychic paradigm,
Aligning, refining, re-defining the mind-monster,
Protecting my introspection.

Rejection of journeying to another trauma pocket dimension,
With positive purpose and intention.
Revealing tenacity,
A deep capacity,
To unpack the cruel,
Release the kind,
Be still in body, gentle mind.

Platitude

Embrace an evolved cerebral plane,
Ingrain the civility of attitudinAll stability,
Platitudinous irradiation,
Quantumplate illumination.

Rash Decisions Open Wounds?

Rash decisions open wounds?
Impulsive decisions of a reactive nature.
Ruminate, hesitate, procrastinate.

People

Courageous people persevere.
Kind people understand.
Compassionate people accept.
Strong people forgive.
Intelligent people ignore.
Weak people revenge.

Successful people endow.
Connected people thrive.
Mature people keep growing.
Vulnerable people love.

Future Me

We cannot know who we might become if we are disconnected from where we come from.

The Phi❣osopher

A philosopher is someone who strives for systematic expertise at working out how one may best find individual and collective fulfillment.

Oceans of the Mind

Bonded by sticky situations,
The Bi-Polarizing-Bi-o-rhythms
of pain.

Reeling,
From emotional feeling,
The cerebral Cathedral
of shame.

Isolated by the confines of the mind,
The kind of blind man seeks relief to find,
Sobering discoveries,
Re-shaping,
Escaping,
The emotional penitentiary,
of blame.

Steps into the light,
Rights on track,
Bright lefts illuminating the blacks,
Shadow memories of the recent past,
Left go at longest last.

Fluctuate, post nuptial,
Firing synapses,
Coping with apocalyptic arenas,
Acropolyptic in scope,
The Gods of Hope,
Scoping out the mind-scape.

Racing thoughts,

Towards chequered-flags,

of diminishing finishing lines,

of unwindable human races.

Chasing head spaces,

Tangential word-salad,

Melodious dead-head places,

Unstable velocities,

Untreated pathologies.

Referencing reverential ammunition,

Fired from Priestly Canons,

Revelationships set sail

on calmer Oceans of the Mind.

EnLighten

When you're tired of living in darkness, turn on the light.
Illuminate the present moment.

The vibrant color wheel of emotional functionability will inspire a spiritual enlightenment of self-unmatched in our experienced lives.

Birth Star

Outer space, inward grace
An inner layer of outward crust.
Needs want must.
Friendly cloudy ozone dust.

Darkly silhouettes of outward luminosity,
Universally viewed through a clouded spot in a cornea,
Visual incision,
Constantly causing defective vision.
Such is the condition,
Of repetition,
Inside a gaseous nebula.

A necessary evil is necessary life.

For a star to be born,
There is one thing that must happen:

A gaseous nebula must collapse.

So collapse.
Crumble.
This is your
destruction.

This is your birth.

The Sands of Time

Rush not the sands of time,
The shifting sense of solemnity,
For the hour is upon us,
It has been,
Before we affected the hourglass of our hearts.

A wise man once regarded,
Is a soul to be regarded,
To impart and bring forth,
That which he never dared to dream of,
To believe in,
The regard for all to see...
The shifting sands of time in our humanity.

The Healing Word

The Feeling World
Hearing feeling words
Feeling heard
Fearing hearing hurtful feeling words
The fearing Feeling of revealing feelings
The Healing

Immaculate Perception

Matriculate your perspective
Emasculate your personification
Metastasize your positivity
Immaculate your perception

Conceptualize your self worth
Craft a new way of thinking
Create a new way of feeling
Urbanize the monastery of your mind.
Aggregate behavior
Regulate emotions

PsychoBabylon

I don't need to disprove the lies you tell yourself about me.
I cannot reveal evidence of who you believe I am when there is none.
This is your voyage of discovery in your own imagination.
You mean me no harm by exposing the lies you tell yourself to believe in.

Uncomfortable truths expunged by the creation of an imagined demigod reside engulfed by the self entangled PsychoBabylon of your demons.

Common Sense

Why is common sense so uncommon? Our behavior so unreasonable?
Self-knowledge affords insight into what we see and think inside our mind's eye.
Sparking intuitive instincts shifts our perspective, enlivens and awakens our self-awareness.
Mindful consciousness empowers our perception to trust in our common senses.
Embracing the negative aspects of life affords us the ability to Feel Life's Touch 👆

The Theocratical Dogma of Mindfulness

Psychological awareness is becoming the organizing religion of western civilization.

Mindusefullness

Psychological land full of the mind.

Everyone dumping 'stuff' into their minds to fill them up. What with? Who cares?

I want to be mindful - filling up my cognitive storage space with information without a learned ability to process through the data.

It's become the new religious doctrine.

The theocratical dogma of mindfulness

Filling up the mind is not enough, or in actuality, may be too much.

We must be aware of what our mind is being 'filled' with and next purpose

Freedom of association with any aspect of the mind fuel.

Mind-fuel-ness ♥✚

Mind-fuel for feelings

Mindfuelings

Mindfeelness

Mindfullplus

Mindfull ✚

Positive mindfeeling

Mindfeelness

Mindfuless

Made in the USA
Columbia, SC
23 September 2020